NOV 2010

WHAT in the WILD?

Mysteries of Nature Concealed . . . and Revealed

EAR-TICKLING POEMS BY **DAVID M. SCHWARTZ & YAEL SCHY**

EYE-TRICKING PHOTOS BY **DWIGHT KUHN**

TRICYCLE PRESS

Berkeley

Introduction

This is a book for people who love mysteries — mysteries in nature. If you would like to be a nature detective, you'll find plenty of cases to crack on these pages. The woods, fields, marshes, rivers, ponds, deserts, farms, and other places are alive with brain teasers waiting to be solved. Welcome to a world of wonder.

Here you will find some odd-looking things — a thick clump of dead leaves in a tree; muddy mounds crisscrossing a lawn; a gob of stuff that looks like bubbles stuck to a stem; a small, compacted pellet of fur and bones lying on the forest floor; a craterlike pit in sandy ground. What are these? That's what you have to figure out. What animal made them? How were they made? What purpose do they serve? The poems on the facing pages will give you hints, but they will not tell you outright. You still have to solve the mysteries yourself.

When you are ready for the answer, lift the flap to get a glimpse of nature's inner workings. You might get to look inside the mystery object, or perhaps you will see the creature that made it. All of these wonders are explained in additional notes. Have a *wonder*ful time.

Lumpy Mounds

These lumpy mounds upon the ground you may not recognize.

They're left behind once we have dined —that's how we fertilize.

We're long and lithe, we wriggle and writhe. Of dead things we dispose.

We daily toil to plow the soil, and help stuff decompose!

Stowaway

hollow sphere on oak

this apple you cannot eat

stowaway within

LIFT TO REVEAL ME!

Star-Nosed Mole

Have you met mild-mannered, lovable Mole from *The Wind in the Willows*? Mole's good-natured personality has won the hearts of millions. Unfortunately, humans rarely view real-life moles with the same affection. Bad feelings toward moles usually begin when people find unsightly heaps of soil in their yard.

Moles spend most of their time underground, excavating elaborate tunnels. With their strong muscles and wide, flat forelegs, they can dig their way through one hundred feet of soil in a single day. In some cases, they push the soil straight up through short vertical tunnels to create volcano-like mounds, or molehills, aboveground. At other times, a mole simply pushes upward all the way along its runway, creating ridges of moist earth directly above the tunnels.

With their pointy noses and giant forelimbs sticking out sideways, all moles are strange-looking, but one kind of mole is truly bizarre. The star-nosed mole looks as though its nose got stamped by a star-shaped cookie cutter. Twenty-two fleshy tentacles fan out from its snout.

Living in wetlands, a star-nosed mole digs through mud, wriggling its tentacles to touch up to ten different objects in a second. It decides in an instant whether each one is yummy (like an earthworm) or yucky (like a slimy piece of wood). Like all mole noses, the star-shaped ones are covered with tiny touch-sensitive bumps called Eimer's organs that help the animals feel their way through the darkness. It is the highly sensitive nose of a star-nosed mole that makes it such a threat to the worms, grubs, and millipedes it loves to eat. The secret of its success is in what its nose knows.

LIFT TO
REVEAL
ME!

Earthworm Castings

Before farmers sow seeds, they plow the soil to improve its texture. The soil becomes loose and spongy. In nature, there are no metal plows. Earthworms are nature's plows.

Long and thin, squirmy and moist, lowly earthworms do mighty work. By "worming" through the earth, wiggling and wriggling right and left, they work the soil like a plow. That alone is a big job, but earthworms do even more. They are decomposers— creatures that consume dead animals and plants.

Without decomposers, the world would be cluttered with dead trees, grass, cows, birds, whales, and everything else that ever walked, swam, flew, or grew. Nutrients would be locked inside these dead things. But decomposers break down dead organisms and let the chemicals in their bodies return to the soil. Thanks to decomposers, the earth is a huge recycling center.

Earthworms are among the most important recyclers. In a single acre of land, up to a million earthworms work tirelessly to turn decaying matter into rich soil by eating rotten fruit, fallen leaves, dead flowers, and animal carcasses. What enters one end of an earthworm eventually goes out the other end. The earthworm's droppings form lumpy piles or mounds called castings.

Worm castings contain minerals and other nutrients from worms' food. These chemicals can be taken up by plants and passed on to animals that eat those plants. Life on earth depends on earthworms!

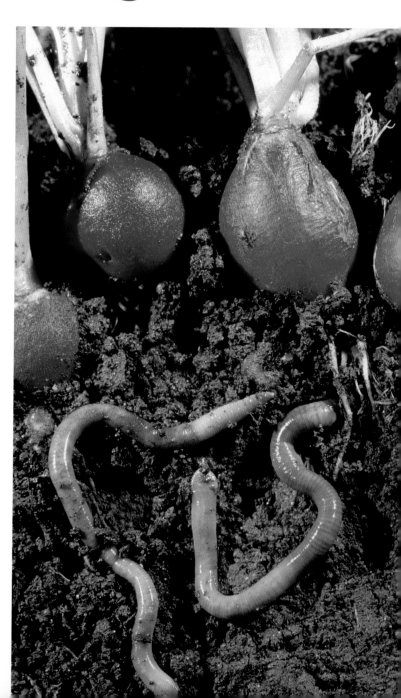

Jaws of a Lion

Walking across the sand, food on my back, almost home—
Oops! The sand is slipping under my feet. . . . No problem, I keep
walking. . . . Wait, I feel myself slipping even more. It's probably
nothing. . . . Uh-oh, I'm slipping faster and faster. HELP! Now I'm
tumbling downhill, falling into the

J e J
A   A
W   W
S   S

of a lion!

LIFT TO
REVEAL
ME!

Antlion Pits

If you don't like scary movies, do not read this page! If you like to be scared, imagine you're taking a stroll down a sandy slope. You notice your feet slipping slightly as the ground steepens. You try to regain your footing, but you lose your balance. You're tumbling into a crater of sand, clawing as you descend. Suddenly, you are pulled into a dark hole. Sharp spikes pierce you, suck out your fluids, and flick you out of the pit.

Don't worry—this will *not* happen to *you*. But if you're an ant or other small insect, watch out! You could easily fall into the pit of an antlion. An antlion is an insect larva that catches prey in funnel-like traps. Its sharp, curved jaws look like sickles and work like hypodermic needles. Antlions live not only in deserts, but also in dunes, riverbanks, and sandy city lots. Some antlion larvae scrape out winding trails in the sand, earning themselves another name: doodlebugs.

Some people keep doodlebugs as pets. Feeding time is quite a show!

Underground

I live underground.

I don't see very well.

To forage for food,

I touch and I smell.

My odd nose is starry.

My sharp claws are big.

By day and by night,

I sniff as I dig.

I make many tunnels,

Pushing dirt aboveground.

To me, it's a mountain—

To you, a small mound!

Cliff Dweller

With expert skill I dive for fish
To serve my young a tasty dish.

With fish that fight, I'm poised for battle,
My telltale voice a throaty rattle.

Atop my head a jagged crest,
I tunnel deep to build my nest.

My home is warm, but kind of smelly
From scraps of fish once in my belly!

Oak Apple Gall

You may have occasionally noticed the leaves of certain trees decorated with papery globes, each about the size of a golf ball. They are tumors—growths that began when the leaf was first forming. A wasp injected its egg into leaf tissue, causing the leaf to form a protective structure around the egg.

Galls are curiosities of the plant kingdom. Inside the gall, wispy fibers radiate outward from the egg like the spokes of a wheel. As the leaf grows, so does the gall. Some grow to a diameter of two inches—large enough to remind people of apples. That is why the galls of some trees are called oak apple galls.

Inside the gall, the wasp egg hatches into a larva, which feeds on leaf tissue. The growing larva fills more and more of the space inside the gall. Eventually it forms a pupa, and finally an adult wasp emerges, escaping to the light of day by boring a hole through the outer wall of the gall.

Although the wasps are taking advantage of the tree, they do not harm it. But the wasps themselves can be in danger from other species of wasps that use their long egg-laying organs, or ovipositors, to probe inside galls, seeking the wasp larvae within. This wasp then lays its own eggs inside a larva. Here's where things get really nasty: When those eggs become larvae, they feed upon the host larva's body tissues. The host wasp will die, eaten from the inside out.

LIFT TO
REVEAL
ME!

LIFT TO
REVEAL
ME!

Kingfisher Burrow

Phew! That hole in the riverbank smells like old fish. You are looking at (and smelling) the burrow of a belted kingfisher, a bird that makes its living pulling fish out of rivers and lakes. When this bird flies, it often gives off a rattling alarm call which many people hear before they see the bird. If you spot one, you will probably first notice the jagged crest of feathers atop its head.

A kingfisher spends much of its time sitting near the water's edge, watching for fish just below the surface. With wings outspread, it dives into water to seize a fish. If the fish fights back, the bird will beat it against a branch before flipping it up and swallowing it, head first.

In the nesting season, kingfishers hammer into a sandy riverbank with their hefty beaks to excavate a deep tunnel where they will nest. If there are no steep-sided banks near the birds' favorite fishing holes, they can dig into a sand pit, dune, or cliff.

At the end of the tunnel, the parents hollow out a chamber. Sometimes they line it with regurgitated fish bones and scales. The female lays about half a dozen round white eggs. When the nestlings hatch, their parents feed them small fish or crustaceans. The nest quickly begins to stink. Scientists have suggested that the stench may help protect eggs and nestlings from predators with sensitive noses!

Blob of Spit

a bulbous, bubbly blob of sticky,

slimy stuff dripping damply

downward, while I

wait and watch,

hunkering and

harbored in my

hidden home

of spit

LIFT TO
REVEAL
ME!

Spittlebug

Imagine walking through a lush meadow on a warm summer day. You notice a small bubbly blob stuck to the stem of a flower. More frothy masses hang from shrubs and tall weeds. They look like foamy gobs of spit! You dare to put a finger into the bubbly mass, and inside you find a pale insect larva.

It is a spittlebug. In its larval stage, this bug spends its time inside a home of spit. But real spit (saliva) comes out of an animal's mouth, while this stuff comes from the other end of its body. Day and night, the mouth of this larva is implanted in the stem of a plant, sucking its juices. As this sap passes through the insect's body, nutrients are absorbed and the remaining liquid is mixed with a substance that makes it thick and slightly sticky. The mixture comes out of the insect's body in the form of bubbles—about eighty per minute—and it becomes a protective "house" for the larva. This moist home helps protect it from predators, extreme temperatures, and the danger of drying out.

In fall, after mating, females lay tiny white eggs inside plant stems. The eggs hatch in the spring, and the larvae, also known as nymphs, immediately make bubbly shelters for themselves. For the next few months they will molt several times, never leaving their moist shelters until they finally molt into adults. Adult spittlebugs are also called froghoppers because of their jumping abilities.

Spittlebugs are often overlooked, but their bubbly homes are hard to miss!

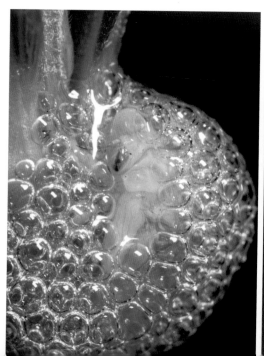

Leafy Lair

Skittery, scattery,

Gathery, chattery—

Stashing my treasures

Where no one can see.

I'm taking no chances—

With leaves, twigs, and branches

I've built a snug nest

High up in a tree.

LIFT TO
REVEAL
ME!

Gray Squirrel nest

What's that tangle of leaves and twigs in the tree? Is it the nest of a large bird? Is it a thick growth of leaves, now dead and brown? Or is it simply a clump of leaves that blew into the tree?

That leafy lair is the home of a mammal well known in cities, suburbs, farmlands, and forests: the gray squirrel. Sometimes squirrels nest in tree holes, but when they can't find a ready-made hole, they make a shaggy-looking nest from dead leaves, twigs, moss, dried grass, strips of tree bark, and just about anything they can find. They even use plastic bags and newspapers! These nests are known as dreys. They protect adult squirrels and their young from predators and the elements.

Gray squirrels may be good architects, but they are bad housekeepers. When the inside of a drey gets too cluttered with twigs and dirt tracked in from the outside, the residents don't clean up the mess. They just move out and build a new drey. Imagine moving to a new house every time yours needs cleaning!

Gray squirrels make different kinds of dreys for winter and summer. Summer dreys are flimsy, but winter dreys are substantial structures built in layers. The outside is made from tough, waterproof materials such as leaves and twigs, but the inner chamber is lined with softer matter—grass, moss, pine needles, and fur that a mother squirrel has plucked from her own belly. In this cozy nest, the squirrel's tiny young—pink and furless—will be born in spring.

Waiting to Break Free

Inside this mass upon a tree
Lie hundreds, waiting to break free.

They'll spend the winter, then they'll hatch
And vie to find a tasty catch.

With patience they will pose and wait,
Then pounce on prey—perhaps a mate!

Praying Mantis Egg Case

Perched in wait for prey, with its triangular head held high and forelegs lifted upward as if in prayer, the praying mantis is easy to recognize. But much less familiar is the walnut-size brown mass stuck to a branch or stalk that contains hundreds of mantis eggs.

In autumn, a female mantis seeks a branch or stalk well above the ground. She hangs upside down and lets a frothy liquid flow from her abdomen. It contains eggs and a material that hardens into a foamy mass that scientists call an *ootheca*, or egg case. Inside, hundreds of eggs pass the winter. As spring approaches, they develop into tiny mantises, or nymphs. Young mantises resemble adults without wings.

Each nymph is enclosed in a transparent membrane that holds its legs tight against its body. Confined to this narrow sack, it looks like a pale worm with large, dark eyes.

With warmer weather, the nymphs wriggle through narrow channels and emerge through slits in the egg case. Dozens of squirming nymphs come cascading out at the same time. Each is trapped inside the sack that had protected it earlier. Dangling upside down from a silk thread, the nymph twists and turns until it breaks through the membrane, then lowers itself to the ground or climbs up the thread. Finally, the young mantis can escape to a nearby tree to look for its first meal.

Regurgitate

I can't digest some things I ate, and so I must regurgitate!

fur, teeth,
bones, skulls,
feathers, beaks, fur,
teeth, bones, skulls,
feathers, beaks . . .
UPCHUCK!

LIFT TO
REVEAL
ME!

Owl Pellets

Owls have very bad table manners. Okay, they don't eat at a table, so let's say that they have bad *tree* manners.

You can sometimes find the evidence beneath an owl's roost. On the ground, you might find several small, dry, rounded masses of—hmm, just what *is* inside these strange-looking things? Look closely. Do you see some familiar bits—fur, bones, maybe some feathers or teeth? You wouldn't want to find these under the kitchen table, but under an owl's roost it's perfectly normal.

Birds cannot chew their food. Instead, they swallow it whole. Raptors (birds of prey such as owls, hawks, and eagles) tear their prey into smaller chunks. In owls, the food goes straight to the stomach, called a gizzard, which acts as a traffic director. It sends the meal in two different directions: nutritious food gets dissolved and continues down the digestive tract, while the hard, indigestible parts are pressed into a rounded pellet and coughed up.

When you find an owl pellet, you are really getting a glimpse into the owl's eating habits. With tweezers, you can pick apart the contents to see what the bird has eaten. You might even be able to reconstruct an entire skeleton from the bones found in the pellet! By examining owl pellets and identifying skulls and other bones, biologists have sometimes discovered prey species not previously known to live in an area.

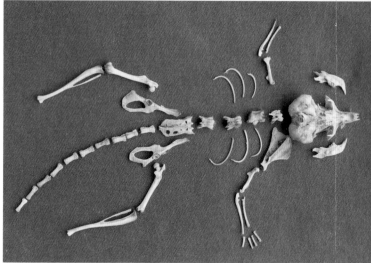

So, no matter what you might think about an owl's table manners, its pellets turn out to be both fascinating and useful. But that doesn't mean you should eat—or cough—like an owl!

Frosty Ring

A frosty ring surrounds this hole,

Revealing I'm inside.

I'm not a mouse, I'm not a mole,

But like them, I must hide

From predators who hunt me down

To catch a tasty bite.

So I dig burrows underground

To keep me out of sight!

LIFT TO
REVEAL
ME!

Meadow Vole

You're walking across a grassy meadow one brisk November morning. Out of the corner of your eye, you detect stirrings in the tall grass—a moving brown blur obscured by the vegetation, now out of sight, then another brownish streak ten feet away. You continue to hike and you notice a small hole in the ground. What catches your eye is the silvery necklace that surrounds it.

You have found a field full of meadow voles. A vole is a small rodent much like mice but a bit larger and chunkier, with a short, hairy tail and rounded nose and ears. Voles eat grass (along with seeds, fruits, roots, and tubers), and they often make runways through high grass. Disappearing into these grass-lined tunnels is their best defense against hawks, owls, snakes, foxes, weasels, and other predators. In winter, they build tunnels in the snow.

But what about that white ring around the small hole in the ground? While voles spend most of their time above the ground, they also dig burrows for food storage and nesting. Females give birth to their young and nurse them underground. They can have several litters each year, from early spring to late fall. On a chilly autumn night, the moist breath of voles in their underground den can condense around the burrow's entrance and freeze in the chill air, giving the hole a frosty ring. Come morning, before the sun melts the ice crystals, you may chance upon the white-rimmed vole hole. Mystery solved!

WE'RE BABY GARDEN SPIDERS!

FOR FURTHER READING

Earthworm: Lauber, Patricia and Todd Telander. *Earthworms: Underground Farmers*. New York: Henry Holt, 1994.

Antlion: Pascoe, Elaine. *Nature Close-Up: Antlions and Lacewings*. San Diego: Blackbirch Press, 2004.

Star-Nosed Mole: Conniff, Richard. *Every Creeping Thing: True Tales of Slightly Repulsive Wildlife*. New York: Henry Holt, 1998.

Oak Apple Gall: David Herlock, "Oak Apple Galls," University of California, Davis, http://cemarin.ucdavis.edu/files/61101.pdf.

Kingfisher: Line, Les. "The Fisher King." *National Wildlife*, June/July 1996.

Spittlebug: Pascoe, Elaine. *Nature Close-Up: Spittlebugs and Other Sap Suckers*. San Diego: Blackbirch Press, 2003.

Squirrel: Peck, George. *Nature's Children: Squirrels*. Danbury, CT: Grolier Academic Reference, 1994.

Praying Mantis: Lavies, Bianca. *Backyard Hunter: The Praying Mantis*. New York: Puffin, 2000.

Owl: Gibbons, Gail. *Owls*. New York: Holiday House, 2005.

Meadow Vole: http://animaldiversity.ummz.umich.edu/site/accounts/information/Microtus_pennsylvanicus.html (1995–2008).

To my husband, David Schwartz,
with deep affection and everlasting love.
—Y.S.

To my cousins, the wonderful Kellehers—
Joci, Mike, Lizzy, and Amy—with affection and appreciation.
—D.M.S.

To my wife, Kathy. You are the greatest!
—D.K.

Text copyright © 2010 by David M. Schwartz and Yael Schy
Photographs copyright © 2010 by Dwight Kuhn

Additional photography credits:
© David Kuhn: Clue Squirrel photo, Support Squirrel photo (bottom), Support Spittlebug photo (right)
© Brian Kuhn: Clue Owl Pellet photo, Support Owl Pellet photo (top), Squirrel Reveal photo

Published in the United States by TRICYCLE PRESS,
an imprint of Random House Children's Books, a division of Random House, Inc., New York.
www.randomhouse.com/kids

Tricycle Press and the Tricycle Press colophon are registered trademarks of Random House, Inc.

Library of Congress Cataloging-in-Publication Data
Schwartz, David M.
What in the wild? : mysteries of nature concealed—and revealed / ear-tickling poems
by David M. Schwartz and Yael Schy ; eye-tricking photos by Dwight Kuhn.—1st ed.
p. cm.
1. Animals—Juvenile literature. I. Schy, Yael. II. Kuhn, Dwight. III. Title.
QL49.S27518 2010
508—dc22   2009043913

ISBN 978-1-58246-310-0 (hardcover)
978-1-58246-359-9 (Gibraltar lib. bdg.)
Printed in China

Design by Lisa Diercks, based on the design by Melissa Brown
Typeset in Fedra Sans and Jacoby

1 2 3 4 5 6 — 14 13 12 11 10